the TRAIL of '42

A Pictorial History of the Alaska Highway

FT. ST. JOHN 48
FT. NELSON 300
WHITEHORSE 922
FAIRBANKS 1568

MILE "0" ALASKA HIGHWAY

Mile "0" Alaska Hwy. Dawson Cr. B.C.

Canada

DEPT. OF PUBLIC WORKS

CONTACT CREEK K/M **945.2**

THIS MARKS THE LOCATION WHERE THE CORPS OF ENGINEERS, U.S. ARMY WORKING FROM THE NORTH MET THOSE WORKING FROM THE SOUTH AND OFFICIALLY OPENED THE ALASKA HIGHWAY, IN OCTOBER 1942. IN 1957, CANADIAN ARMY ENGINEERS REPLACED THE ORIGINAL TIMBER BRIDGE WITH THE PRESENT STRUCTURE.

the TRAIL of '42

A Pictorial History of the Alaska Highway

by STAN COHEN

PICTORIAL HISTORIES PUBLISHING CO.
MISSOULA, MONTANA

LIBRARY OF CONGRESS
CATALOG CARD NUMBER 79-51360

ISBN 0-933126-06-9

First Printing: June 1979
Second Printing: February 1980
Third Printing: February 1981
Fourth Printing: February 1982
Fifth Printing: April 1983
Sixth Printing: March 1984
Seventh Printing: April 1985
Eighth Printing: April 1986
Ninth Printing: April 1987
First Revised Printing: May 1988
Second Revised Printing: April 1989
Third Revised Printing: March 1990

Typography: Arrow Graphics, Missoula, Montana

Printed by Friesen Printers
Altona, Manitoba, Canada

PICTORIAL HISTORIES PUBLISHING CO.
713 South Third West
Missoula, Montana 59801

PREFACE

*A*nyone who travels the Alaska Highway today for the first time would be hard put to imagine the hardships associated with the building of the road. Today one whizzes by on a paved highway in modern cars, trucks and campers, past clean modern motels, cafes and towns. In the early 1940s this was mostly wilderness, traveled by a small band of hunters, trappers and prospectors and several Indian tribes. The mile upon mile of desolate countryside and harsh weather conditions continued to make this area hostile to modern development. Even today, the road can be very inhospitable at times and the area just off the highway is still very remote and rugged.

We can thank in part the cooperation of the United States and Canadian governments for building the road and bringing it to the condition it is in now for the tourist traveling to Canada and Alaska. It has undoubtedly vastly increased the modernization of the North Country, which may in fact be considered a sin to some of the old-timers in the area.

It is hoped that this pictorial history will give the traveler an idea of what these men had to face in the early 1940s. It is difficult now to put the entire story in perspective. The photographs were selected from various archives in the United States and Canada to show not only the road construction, but something of the way the soldiers and construction men lived.

Since the publication of this volume in 1979 the highway has been paved and much development has occurred along the way. The 50th anniversary of the pioneer road is fast approaching. Many new photographs have surfaced, some used in this revised edition.

I wish to thank the staff members of the following archives who helped in my search for photographs: National Archives, Library of Congress; United States Army; Provincial Archives of Alberta; Provincial Archives of British Columbia; Yukon Archives; Glenbow Archives; South Peace River Historical Society; and the Alaska Historical Library. Many thanks to Garth Hall, Dawson Creek; Earl Brown, Ft. Nelson; Dedman's Photo Shop, Skagway; Phylis Bowman, Prince Rupert; Dorothy Jones, Forest Grove, Oregon; and Carl Lindley, Danville, Illinois, for their help with photos and information. Also to the dozens of other people I have talked to through the years who worked on the highway.

This book is dedicated to those men who opened up a wonderful part of our continent for the enjoyment of all who want to seek its wonders.

Stan Cohen

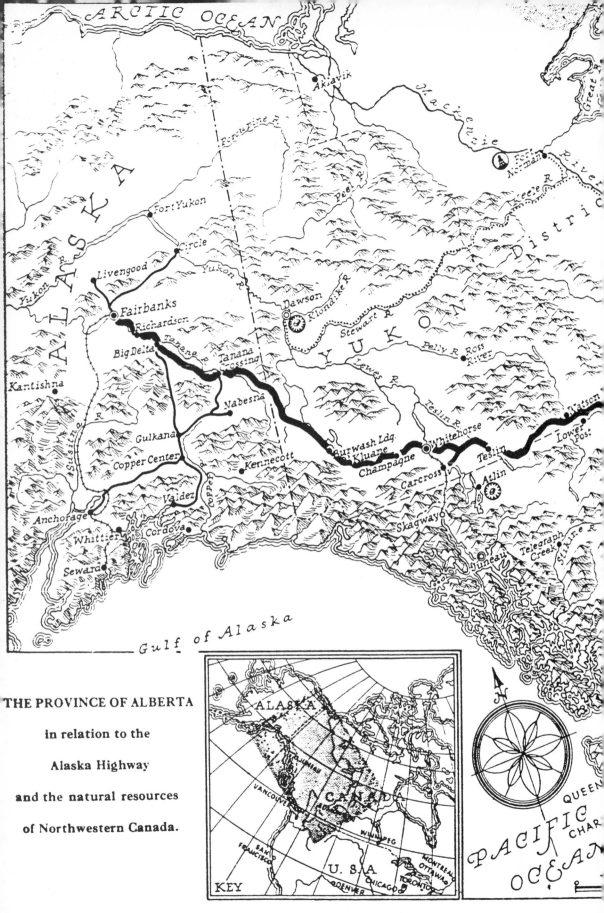

ARCTIC OCEAN

Akiavik

Mackenzie

Fort Norman

Porcupine R.

Keele R.

Peel R.

District

Fort Yukon

Circle

Livengood

Yukon R.

Fairbanks

Richardson

Big Delta

Tanana R.

Tanana Crossing

Dawson

Klondike R.

Stewart R.

YUKON

Pelly R.

Ross River

Lewes R.

Teslin R.

Watson L.

Kantishna

Susitna R.

Nabesna

Gulkana

Copper Center

Valdez

Copper R.

Kennecott

Burwash Ldg.
Kluane

Champagne

Whitehorse

Teslin

Lower Post

Anchorage

Whittier

Cordova

Carcross

Atlin

Skagway

Seward

Telegraph Creek

Juneau

Stikine R.

Gulf of Alaska

THE PROVINCE OF ALBERTA

in relation to the

Alaska Highway

and the natural resources

of Northwestern Canada.

ALASKA

CANADA

VANCOUVER

SAN FRANCISCO

WINNIPEG

MONTREAL
OTTAWA

DENVER

CHICAGO

TORONTO

U.S.A.

KEY

N

PACIFIC

QUEEN

CHAR

OCEAN

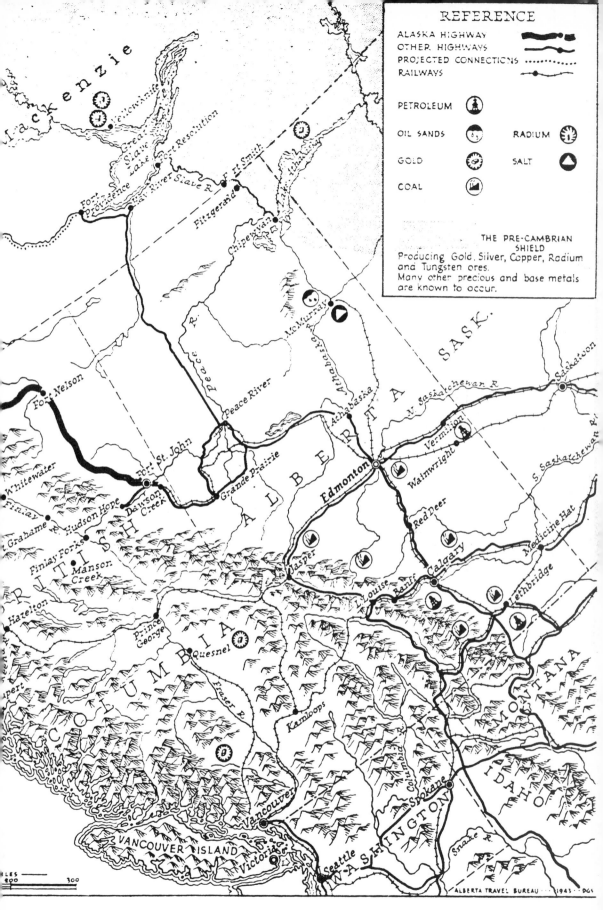

CONTENTS

PHOTOGRAPH ABBREVIATIONS

USA	United States Army Archives, Washington, D.C.
LC	Library of Congress, Washington, D.C.
NA	National Archives, Washington, D.C.
AHL	Alaska Historical Library, Juneau
GA	Glenbow Archives, Calgary, Alberta
SPRHS	South Peace River Historical Society, Dawson Creek
YA	Yukon Archives, Whitehorse
GH	Garth Hall Collection, Dawson Creek
PABC	Public Archives of British Columbia, Victoria
PAA	Provincial Archives of Alberta-Edmonton
SC	Author's Collection

Other photos credited to the source.

EARLY HIGHWAY PROPOSALS

*T*he dream of an overland route to Alaska was thought of long before the Second World War. A veteran American railroad builder, F.H. Harriman, proposed a Canada-Alaska railroad linked with a Russian railroad by bridging or tunneling the Bering Straits. However, after Japan defeated Russia in the Russo-Japanese War of 1904, she pressured Russia into abandoning the idea.

In 1905, Major Constantine of the North West Mounted Police was ordered to blaze an overland trail to the Klondike gold fields. He started from Ft. St. John and got to the Stikine River before he was ordered back. He had built 375 miles of road.

Donald MacDonald, a United States government engineer, proposed an overland road to Alaska in 1928. His thoughts were to link Alaska and the Polar Seas with Panama. This route could be used for military purposes but the country was not interested in military considerations at that time.

In 1933 the United States Congress authorized President Roosevelt to set up a joint commission with Canada to study a proposed road to Alaska. There was no action by this commission by 1938 other than to name new members. They were Congressman Warren Magnuson of Washington; Ernest Gruening of Alaska; Donald MacDonald of Alaska; F.W. Carey, the Public Works Administrator of Oregon; and Thomas Riggs, ex-governor of Alaska. The Canadian commissioners were Charles Stewart, Brig. Gen. Thomas Tremblay, J.M. Wardle, Arthur Dixon and J.W. Spencer.

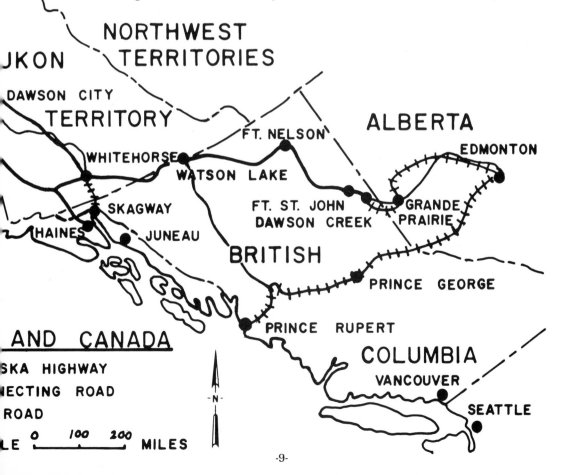

View of the Chilkoot Barracks at Haines, Alaska during the war—This was an early U.S. Army post in Alaska, established in 1904 and originally called Ft. Wm. H. Seward. The name was later changed to Port Chilkoot. Haines was the southern terminus of the Haines Cutoff highway, built in 1943 to provide another access into the interior of Alaska and Canada. USA

ALASKAN AND CANADIAN DEFENSES

After the purchase of Alaska from Russia in 1867, various military units were stationed in the southeast section for years. Gold was discovered in the Juneau area in the 1880s and more strikes were made in the Klondike in 1896, at Nome in 1899 and in Fairbanks in the early 1900s. The need for more civil and military presence was apparent. Troops were stationed at several military posts in Alaska including Chilkoot Barracks at Haines. Other units went into the interior to set up a communications system.

By 1940 there were over 72,000 people in Alaska and it was apparent that not only was Alaska a vital gateway to Canada and the west coast of the United States but its defenses were sorely lacking. Russia was reported to be building an air base on Big Diomede Island only one and one-half miles from Alaska and the infamous Gen. Billy Mitchell had warned for years of a possible Japanese attack.

The first major contingent of American troops arrived at Anchorage in the spring of 1940 and a submarine and air base were built at Sitka in southeastern Alaska along with air bases at Fairbanks, Anchorage and Kodiak. The naval base at Dutch Harbor in the Aleutian Islands was strengthened.

After the fall of France in June 1940, the United States and Canada set up a Canadian-American Permanent Joint Board of Defense in August to oversee all defense policies for both countries. This included approving the Northwest Staging Route air bases and the Alaska Highway.

The Japanese were greatly disturbed by the American defense moves as shown in a newspaper article in 1941.

Japan Greatly Disturbed Over Proposed Highway To Alaska From United States

The newspaper *Hochi* stated today that Japan is greatly disturbed over reported plans for building a military highway from the United States to Alaska through western Canada. The newspaper said that the Tokyo foreign office was informed that a string of air bases will be built along the highway by the United States and Canadian governments.

Hochi declared "American measures in this direction will be regarded as a continuation of the horseshoe-shaped encirclement of Japan by the Washington Government. Military bases of the United States would thus be strategic from Singapore via Australia, the Phillipines, Hawaii and the United States to Canada and Alaska."

Even with this increased military activity, Alaska was open to surprise attack as the United States was drawn into the war in December 1941.

NORTHWEST STAGING ROUTE

With the beginning of the Second World War in September 1939 Canada began to look at its own defense posture. The defense of western Canada, and to a degree Alaska and the western United States, was the main reason a string of air bases extending from Edmonton, Alberta to Fairbanks, Alaska was proposed to be built. The purpose of those bases was to facilitate the movement of aircraft and supplies to western Canada and Alaska. In early 1941, bases were constructed in Grande Prairie, Alberta; Ft. Nelson, British Columbia; and Watson Lake and Whitehorse, Yukon Territory. The existing Ladd Field at Fairbanks, Alaska was expanded as the northern terminus of the air route. Bases were also built at Prince George and Smithers, British Columbia.

This air route followed one pioneered by Grant McConachie and his Yukon Southern Air Transport in the 1930s.

The Northwest Staging Route, as it was to become known, had two very important functions during the war. First, it not only was the main factor in locating the highway along the present route, but it was very useful in the highway construction. Second the airfields were used a great deal by American pilots ferrying planes to Fairbanks to be picked up by Russian crews for lend-lease to Russia.

P-40 fighter planes lined up at the Northwest Staging Route airfield at Ft. Nelson in April, 1942. The highway connected the airfields at Ft. St. John, Ft. Nelson, Watson Lake, Whitehorse and Fairbanks. USA

PROPOSED ROUTES

Several routes had been proposed for the road before and after construction was authorized.

The Americans were proponents of Route A which started in central British Columbia at Prince George, then moved northwest to Hazelton, up the Stikine River to Altin to Teslin and Tabish lakes, to Whitehorse and Fairbanks via the Tanana Valley. The route would connect Alaska and Seattle and parallel the west coast for 150 miles but it was vulnerable to possible enemy attack from the sea, had steep grades and heavy snowfall and there were no air bases along the way.

The Canadians favored Route B which also started at Prince George but which followed the Rocky Mountain Trench up the valleys of the Parsnip and Finlay rivers to Finlay Forks and Syton Pass, then north to Francis Lake in the Yukon to the Pelly River. From there it went to Dawson City and down the Yukon Valley to connect the Richardson Highway to Fairbanks. The advantage of this route was that it was farther inland—away from enemy planes, but again there were no connecting air bases. Also Whitehorse, the most important town in the Yukon, was bypassed. Construction cost was estimated at $25 million with a time factor of five to six years.

Vihjalmur Stefansson, the pioneer Arctic explorer, had proposed a Mackenzie River route from Great Slave Lake in the Northwest Territories up the Mackenzie River, across the Yukon to Eagle, Alaska and Fairbanks. This route was impractical from its inception due to the remoteness of the area.

As it turned out the so-called Prairie Route (Route C), advocated by the United States Army Corps of Engineers, was the only practical one. It was far enough inland to avoid attack by enemy planes from the sea and it connected the vital air bases of the Northwest Staging Route from Edmonton to Fairbanks. It traversed through more level terrain, not ascending a pass over 4,250 feet. There was also a railhead at Dawson Creek, British Columbia and a winter trail from there to Fort Nelson, 300 miles to the northwest. Another access point was through Skagway, Alaska.

The road, when completed, traversed over 1,400 miles from Dawson Creek to its junction with the Richardson Highway at Delta Junction, Alaska.

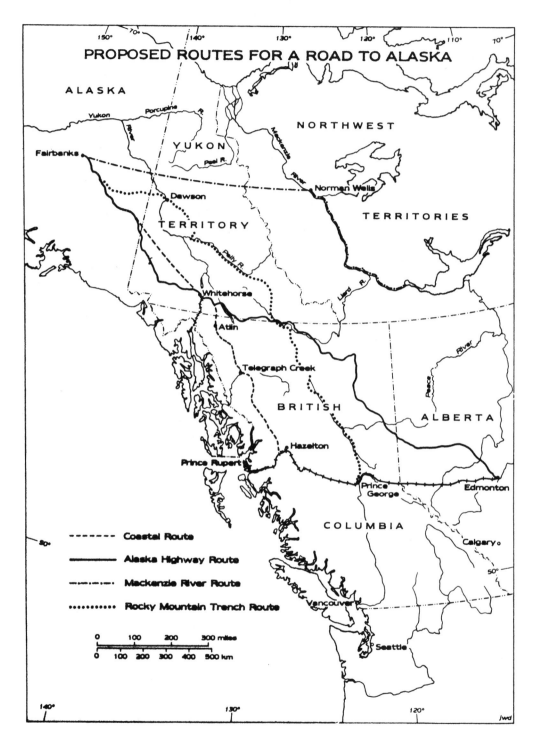

PROPOSED ROUTES FOR A ROAD TO ALASKA

- `------` Coastal Route
- `———` Alaska Highway Route
- `—·—·—` Mackenzie River Route
- `··········` Rocky Mountain Trench Route

MAP FROM *THE ALASKA HIGHWAY, PAPERS OF THE 40TH ANNIVERSARY SYMPOSIUM,* UNIVERSITY OF BRITISH COLUMBIA PRESS.

INITIAL CONSTRUCTION

The bombing of Pearl Harbor on December 7, 1941 was to produce one of the great engineering feats of the century. The west coast of the United States and Canada and all of Alaska lay open to a possible Japanese invasion and the defense of the area was of paramount importance in the early days of the war.

The attack had prompted President Roosevelt to form the Special Cabinet Committee to study the problems of building a road to Alaska through Canada. Brig. Gen. C.L. Sturdevant, the Assistant Chief of the United States Army Corps of Engineers, was detailed to put together plans for the road's actual construction at the earliest possible time. There was opposition to building the road even after Pearl Harbor. The navy thought it could keep the sea lanes free of enemy intrusions and the army questioned the use of badly needed supplies and soldiers on such a large scale project. But the pressing need for a quick decision to get men and supplies to the area while the ground was still frozen prompted action. After much haggling over which route to follow, a decision was made on Feb. 2, 1942 to follow Route C or the Prairie Route. On February 14 a directive was issued for actual work to begin.

The plan was to start a road from the end of the railroad at Dawson Creek, British Columbia, cutting a pioneer road suitable only for military traffic to Whitehorse and terminating at Fairbanks, Alaska. It was to be built as fast as possible. Later it was to be followed up as a year around road with wider roadbeds and permanent bridges built by the United States Public Roads Administration (PRA).

Arrangements had to be made with the Canadian government, as most of the road would be built through British Columbia and the Yukon Territory, using American troops and equipment. The Canadians agreed to furnish the right of way, to waive import duties, sales taxes, income taxes and immigration regulations and to permit the taking of timber, gravel and rock from crownlands along the route. The Americans agreed to pay for the construction and to turn over the Canadian portion of the road to the Canadian government six months after the war ended.

The initial command of the construction project was in the hands of Gen. William M. Hoge, who tried to control the entire length of the route. He set up a southern sector headquarters at Ft. St. John and a northern sector headquarters at Whitehorse. This arrangement did not work due to the scope of the project and in June General Hoge assumed command of the northern sector. Col. James A. O'Connor took over the southern sector. O'Connor, a 1907 West Point graduate, was the engineer in charge of tunneling Corregidor's fortress in Manila harbor. Due to a lack of control over the entire project and to supply problems, a Northwest Service Command was established in September 1942 in Whitehorse with O'Connor, now a general, in charge. The Command was in charge of all U.S. Army activities along the highway and in that part of Canada.

By the first week of February, the President had authorized the army to proceed with all haste to begin construction of the road. It was initially named the Alcan Highway. Emergency funds were allocated and orders were issued to army troops to proceed to the end of rail at Dawson Creek. On March 2, 1942 the first train carrying troops arrived at the town.

Pack trains were used extensively in the early construction period to take supplies to the surveyors marking out the road right-of-way ahead of the construction crews. YA

Pack trains moving through muddy paths at MP 48.0, June 25, 1942. USA

Advance survey party, 1942. GA

The end of the rail line was at Dawson Creek ... s of supplies and equipment and thousands of troops were brought ... Alberta Railroad. LC

Members of the 341st Engineers stake out ... e at Dawson Creek, May, 1942. USA

There were few reliable maps of the proposed route and a few trails cut by the local trappers and prospectors. There was a winter trail from Dawson Creek to Ft. Nelson and a wagon road from Whitehorse northwest to Kluane Lake, but not much more.

The 35th Combat Engineers were ordered to proceed to Dawson Creek and then to Ft. Nelson to begin location work in the spring. The 340th General Service Regiment went to Whitehorse and was to build the road south. The 341st General Service Regiment was stationed at Ft. St. John and was to build the road to Ft. Nelson. The 18th Combat Engineer Regiment went to Skagway and traveled the railroad to Whitehorse to build the road northwest toward Alaska.

Those four regiments were thus poised in the spring of 1942 for the great construction job ahead. Twelve hundred miles of road in Canada and over 200 miles in Alaska were to be cut through as quickly as possible. With the addition of three more army regiments, the 93rd, 95th and 97th—all of which were composed of black troops with white officers—the total strength of troops for the construction job in 1942 was over 11,000. The PRA also provided location crews and private contractors during this period.

Dawson Creek in early March was swarming with troops starting up the "road" to Ft. St. John and Ft. Nelson. The road was to follow the winter trail from Ft. St. John past Charlie Lake through thick forests and along ridgetops on the eastern slopes of the Rocky Mountains, crossing several large rivers and continuing to Ft. Nelson.

Gov. Ernest Gruening of Alaska, second from left, visited the Public Roads Administration camp in Whitehorse in October, 1942. On the left is Brig. Gen. James J. O'Connor, Commanding General of the highway construction. Third from left is Col. John Wheeler, in charge of the actual construction and to his right is Col. K. Bush, Chief of Staff. NA

Original headquarters of the Southern sector, early 1942, at Ft. St. John. LC

American officers stand in front of the Whitehorse sector headquarters, June, 1942. USA

Surveying to lay out a line for the bulldozers to follow through the dense forest was difficult but necessary. The center line was roughed out on maps but the foot-by-foot line had to be surveyed and investigated on the ground. Members of the 341st Engineers survey between Ft. St. John and Ft. Nelson in May, 1942. USA

The advance survey and construction crews set up bases along the highway route. This photo shows a cook tent for the officers' mess near Carcross, Yukon Territory in July, 1942. USA

The very dense stands of timber had to be cleared by bulldozers. USA

Sometimes the only thing that could get through was horsepower and even that was difficult. The scene is near Sanpete Creek. NA

Local trappers, Indians and prospectors were pressed into service to help locate the way, although their suggestions for possible routes were not always the most appropriate for a motorized highway. Local packers with their mule teams were used to help supply the advanced survey parties.

Three hundred thirty-five miles of wilderness stretched from Ft. Nelson to Watson Lake, the first settlement in the Yukon Territory. The highest point of the road crossed Summit Lake at over 4,000 feet. The road then traversed up the mountains and down valleys, crossing large rivers and hundreds of small streams. The road followed a general northwesterly direction to Watson Lake. Names such as Trutch, Steamboat Mountain, Toad River, Muncho Lake and the Liard River were etched forever in the minds of the soldiers who labored on the road.

At Lower Post, just south of the Yukon border, the new road followed an old road to Watson Lake, where the route to the northwest was very unclear. Several routes to Whitehorse were explored and the one finally chosen followed the Rancheria River Valley across the Mackenzie-Yukon River divide, then along the Swift River to Teslin Lake and Marsh Lake. It followed an old prospector's trail to Whitehorse.

From Whitehorse, the road skirted the north side of the St. Elias Range, around the south shore of Kluane Lake, the largest in the Yukon, and crossed the large glacial rivers of western Yukon—the Slims, the Donjek and the White. At the Alaska border, over 1,200 miles from Dawson Creek, the route traversed through the Tanana River Valley connecting Northway and Tok to Delta Junction where the road connected with the Richardson Highway, built in the 1920s. Delta Junction is recognized by some and Fairbanks by others as the official end of the highway.

The soldiers of the army and the civilians of the PRA faced countless days of below

An engineer chopping through the permanently frozen soil that was present along the road route. Road building of this magnitude had never before been attempted in this country and it took quite a while to figure out how to deal with the unusual soil conditions. NA

One of the first camps along the highway route. A sawmill supplied building materials and wood for fires. LC

zero temperatures, snow, rain, insects and even intense heat coupled with the problems associated with building a road in an unknown environment.

By April road locaters were working throughout the country with the hum of bulldozers on their heels. Decisions on the route were sometimes made on the spot and if the route was not quite in the right place, the PRA men corrected it later. Workers often climbed trees to figure out the route ahead. Then the bulldozers would cut out a path. Often three to four miles of road were built in a day as the summer daylight hours permitted the men to work 24 hours a day. The big push was to get to Fairbanks as soon as possible with a pioneer road. Local bush pilots were hired to ferry men and supplies along the route. The riverboats along the Yukon's inland rivers and lakes were pressed into service. There was no limit set on the amount of equipment or money to get the job done. To the old-timers of the north, this American explosion of power and wealth was overwhelming.

There was a race against time in the southern sector as spring thaws made travel over the winter trail in the Ft. St. John to Ft. Nelson area impossible. Supplies had to be stockpiled on the route for the spring and summer construction period.

The most pressing problem along the route was the inexperience of the engineers in building a highway on the muskeg and permafrost. The ground is permanently frozen year around just below the muskeg in many areas along the route and if the top layer is stripped off, which was the case along part of the route, the underlying ground thaws out and produces a quagmire which is difficult to deal with. Ditches were installed to drain off the excess thawing water, but were ineffective. Finally the crews left the muskeg intact and built the road on top of it, laying a roadbed of gravel where needed.

Laying corduroy roads in areas of extremely swampy conditions—It was found early in construction that if the topsoil was stripped off, the underlying permafrost would thaw out and create impassable conditions. USA

Members of the 95th Engineers lay a corduroy road at MP 15.0, June, 1942. USA

A portable sawmill set up near Ft. Nelson—it could be used to cut deck planking and other lumber products at the job site. PABC

Horses were used on this section of road along Muncho Lake to haul away the blasted rock. NA

The construction methods took a terrific toll in men and machines and there were bound to be accidents along the way. One of the worst tragedies occurred at Charlie Lake near St. John on May 14, 1942. Eleven men drowned in the lake when their raft capsized. Other men were killed in road accidents or died from the extremely cold temperatures.

The route between Whitehorse and the Alaska border was extremely difficult to work on. There was no adequate route information and the terrain was very difficult to cut a road through. There were miles of swamps, large glacial rivers to cross and much hard rock construction—especially around Kluane Lake. Ice jams in the rivers during the spring breakup were very dangerous. The temperatures in winter fell to 50 degrees below zero and lower. At this temperature, machinery would not function and it was very dangerous to work outside. But the work continued through the early spring, summer and fall, with the road slowly being inched toward Alaska. The troops were building both north and south of Whitehorse, the major supply point of the northern sector, and toward Whitehorse from Ft. Nelson. Additional troops of the 97th Engineers proceeded north from Valdez, Alaska and started building the road southeast to the Yukon border. The PRA and the Alaska Road Commission personnel also worked to improve the Richardson Highway into Fairbanks.

Finally on Sept. 24, 1942, bulldozer operators of the 35th and 340th Regiments met at Contact Creek (MP 588.1, Km 946.3) to close the southern sector of the road at Beaver Creek, Yukon (MP 1,202, Km 1,934) on Oct. 20, 1942, when troops working south from Alaska and north from Whitehorse met. Thus the pioneer road had been

The use of wood stave culverts was widespread along the highway route. Wooden boxes, steel pipe and even old oil drums—whatever was available—were also used. NA

completed in record time (eight months and 12 days) and an opening ceremony was held at Soldiers Summit on Kluane Lake on Nov. 20, 1942 to officially celebrate the completion of an overland link to northern Canada and Alaska. General O'Connor represented the United States Army and Minister Ian Mackenzie represented Canada along with a contingent of Royal Canadian Mounted Police and American soldiers. This had been a joint effort of the United States and Canada that probably would have been years off if not sparked by wartime emergencies.

But this was only the beginning as the pioneer road was just that—a partially single lane, very rough road that would have to be upgraded immediately in order to be usable by the increasing military traffic.

Steamboat Mountain, west of Fort Nelson, one of the prominent points along the highway route. GA

"The Grand Canyon of the Alaska Highway"—located north of Whitehorse—so named because it was a ditch formed by the thawing of the frozen silt and the gradual draining of the frozen muck. The passage of equipment only aggravated the almost impossible situation. Conditions at places like this would close the road for days at a time. NA

This 40-mile section of highway from Pickhandle Lake to Beaver Creek was the great bottleneck in the highway. It was impassable until the late summer of 1943 and not completely opened until October, 1943. It was pioneered and traveled in the winter of 1942 but by spring the road had disappeared due to thawing action. Convoys had to be pulled through this section; then they followed the ditches to more solid ground. NA

Construction camp along Summit Lake, the highest point on the road. NA

The road skirts Kluane Lake, a lake 50 miles in length at the base of the St. Elias Range in the lower Yukon. In this section many miles of rock had to be blasted away along the lake shore.
PABC

Facsimiles of the Burma Shave signs were put up along the road. This one says "This Road—Will Lead—The Japs—To Hell—So Build—It Quick—And Build—It Well—Buy Burma Shave." NA

Mud was the constant enemy of the road builders. How could one travel faster than five miles per hour? This photo shows the result of a three day rain. NA

Troops getting a free ride through the mud on an improvised raft. USA

A great catastrophe occurred in the Tokhim River. A 4-ton Diamond T truck loaded with beer for a July 4th party dropped off the barge. Let us hope it was salvaged. YA

Another victim of bad road conditions. USA

A very primitive road between Whitehorse and Kluane Lake. GA

Flooding was a constant problem during the spring thaw conditions. SPRHS

Submerged truck 160 miles north of Fort Nelson. GA

The pioneer road was built without much regard to grades. This would be corrected by the follow-up construction crews. Four wheel drive was a must for this stretch of the road. USA

NEW YORK 3600
CHICAGO 2700
EDMONTON 1215
LOWER POST 15
WATSON LAKE 8
LIARD RIVER 8
WHITEHORSE
TESLIN 172
TOKYO 4000

SPRHS

The construction process was very hard on equipment. SPRHS

A sign erected at the bottom of Suicide Hill, a steep grade that caused many accidents. PAA

Lower Post was a small settlement just east of Watson Lake. AHL

A jeep drives over the rough pioneer corduroy road early in the construction process. LC

The highway runs along Teslin Lake in winter. NA

The first convoy of trucks traveled from Whitehorse to Fairbanks in late November, 1942, eight months after construction had begun. YA

SOLDIERS SUMMIT

Opening ceremonies of the highway at Soldiers Summit, a stretch of the highway 1,500 feet above the wide swath of Kluane Lake, approximately 100 miles east of the Alaska-Yukon international boundary, Nov. 20, 1942. LC

The author's wife at the site of Soldiers Summit, 1987.

The author stands at the site of Soldiers Summit, 1987.

SOLDIERS' SUMMIT

FEBRUARY, 1942 SAW THE BEGINNINGS OF A MILITARY ROAD THAT
WOULD CROSS 2253 KILOMETRES OF WILDERNESS AND PROVIDE A
STRATEGIC LINK TO ALASKA. IT WAS A MASSIVE PROJECT,
WITH SEVEN REGIMENTS OF THE ARMY ENGINEERS AND PRIVATE
CONTRACTORS WORKING NIGHT AND DAY. AS THEY PUNCHED A
PRIMITIVE TRAIL THROUGH THE COUNTRY, THE TROOPS HAD TO
CONTEND WITH MUSKEG, MOSQUITOES AND MUD, AS WELL AS
WEATHER SO COLD THAT IT FROZE THEIR SUPPLY OF ANTIFREEZE.
BY OCTOBER, THE NINETY-SEVENTH ENGINEERS, WORKING EAST,
REACHED THE EIGHTEENTH ENGINEERS, WORKING WEST, AND THE
PIONEER ROAD WAS COMPLETE. A FORMAL CEREMONY WAS HELD
HERE ON NOVEMBER 20, 1942, TO COMMEMORATE THE INCREDIBLE
ACHIEVEMENT OF THOSE TEN MONTHS.

Yukon

KEEPING THE SUPPLIES COMING

*O*ne of the main problems of building the road was keeping the supplies moving toward the construction activity. This is the age old problem in wartime and the process was further complicated by adverse weather conditions, remoteness of the area and the lack of enough ships for the supplies needed.

Whitehorse was the major supply point during the course of construction. Material was moved over the White Pass and Yukon Railway, was trucked toward Whitehorse from the Richardson Highway, and was brought up the road from the south as construction progressed.

Dawson Creek at the end of the railroad was the major supply point for the southern sector. The interior highways of Alaska and the Alaska Railroad connecting Anchorage and Fairbanks kept the goods moving into Alaska. Prince Rupert, British Columbia on the Pacific coast, was also a major supply shipping point to Skagway, Alaska.

Several of the large Yukon lakes were used to supply construction areas along the way by riverboat, and the airplane was used whenever possible. Another access was just north of Edmonton, Alberta, down the Mackenzie River route. This mainly served the CANOL oil field project on the Mackenzie River at Norman Wells, Northwest Territories. A road and pipeline were built from there to connect with the Alaska Highway at Johnson's Crossing (MP 835.7, Km 1,344.9) and then to the refinery at Whitehorse. This project was intended to provide an adequate oil supply for the interior air bases and the Alaska Highway.

Once the pioneer road was completed, the theory was that truck convoys could travel along the road from Dawson Creek to Fairbanks. Actually, so much of the road was closed due to construction problems in 1942 and 1943 that the projected amount of supplies to be moved along the road never materialized.

Canadian Department of Transport ferry on Peace River, at Taylor Flats, British Columbia, May, 1942. GA

USA

Lack of bridges at the time necessitated travel by ferry over many northern rivers. This is the Peace River in Alberta. USA

The *Keno*, an old workhorse on the Yukon and Stewart
rivers is now on display at Dawson City, Yukon. USA

Smaller boats were also put into service. LC

A mail plane of Canadian Pacific Airlines deposits its load at Dawson Creek. SPRHS

Seaplanes on Charlie Lake, a Bellanca and Norseman. GA

Aircraft were used extensively for reconnaisance and supply along the highway route. This float plane landed along the shore of Kluane Lake, summer 1942. YA

The airplane played a vital role in the road construction. Supplies and personnel could be ferried back and forth quickly along the route. The numerous lakes and rivers along the way made float planes highly desirable. NA

Trucks on the highway at the White Pass crossings near Whitehorse, 1944. USA

Trucks hauled tons of supplies on sections of the road that were open to traffic. AHL

SPRHS

A typical "gas station" along the highway in March, 1942. Jerry cans are being filled from 55 gallon drums to be carried in the army trucks along the route. PAA

With sufficient imagination and transport facilities, nothing was too big to haul. River ferries played an important part in the shipment of material along the construction route. This 25,000 gallon tank was ferried across Peace River to be used to fuel highway machines in August, 1942. USA

WHITE PASS AND YUKON RAILWAY

*T*he narrow gauge ribbon of steel that wound its way 110 miles northward from Skagway in Alaska, to Whitehorse in the Yukon Territory, was a very important transportation link long before a highway was thought of and before the military importance of the North Country was realized.

The railroad was constructed in the waning years of the famous Klondike gold rush for the single purpose of getting supplies and prospectors to the goldfields without the grueling foot journey over the White and Chilkoot passes. It was built without the benefit of modern machines through some of the most rugged country on the continent in the narrow gauge width of three feet. No one dreamed at that time that this little railroad would be called upon to supply thousands of tons of material for a war effort 42 years later.

In the years between the world wars, the railroad barely maintained operations due to lagging mineral production in the Yukon and the depression of the 1930s. In the early 1940s the equipment and track were in a state of disrepair. The railroad was not ready for war. There were fewer than a dozen engines that were operational and the roadbed needed to be upgraded.

The Canadian government leased the entire railroad to the United States government for the duration of the conflict. This was contrary to Canadian law, but the war took precedence. On Oct. 1, 1942, the 770th Railway Operating Battalion of the United States Army officially assumed control of operations of the railroad, retaining the railroad's civilian workers.

The lack of equipment was apparent and several engines were shipped from the United States. Even one of the old engines from the defunct railroad that ran to the Klondike gold fields was pressed into service. In 1943, 10 engines destined for railroad service in Iran were diverted to Skagway.

During the war, the railroad accumulated 36 engines and almost 300 freight cars, most of the rolling stock belonging to the United States Army. In 1943 alone the railroad hauled over 280,000 tons of material, compared to 25,000 tons from October to December of 1942. That was in spite of some of the worst weather in history which struck the railroad during the winters of 1942-43 and 1943-44. In 1943 weather closed the line for 10 days and again for 18 days in 1944.

Skagway became another boom town with thousands of troops passing through. The dock facilities were totally inadequate to handle the supplies coming in by ship and the whole area was bursting at the seams.

The railroad company also operated a number of sternwheelers on the Yukon River and inland lakes in the Yukon. Those gave valuable service for the shipment of supplies to remote areas along the highway route.

After the war was over, the railroad was returned to its former operators. It had done its work well and had contributed to the successful completion of the Alaska Highway and the Allied victory.

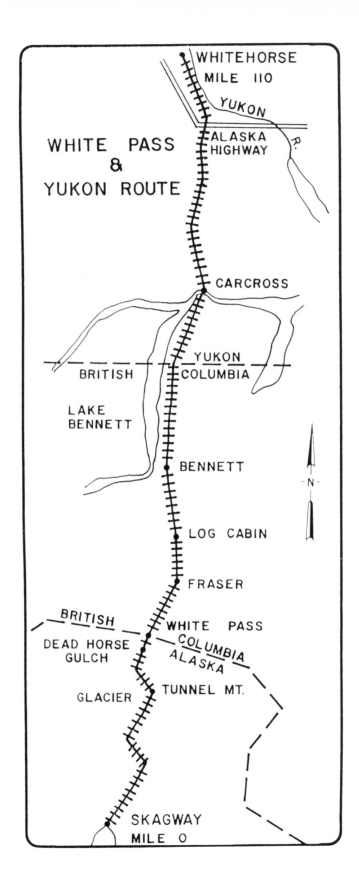

WHITE PASS
&
YUKON ROUTE

WHITEHORSE
MILE 110

YUKON

ALASKA
HIGHWAY

R.

CARCROSS

YUKON
BRITISH COLUMBIA

LAKE
BENNETT

BENNETT

N

LOG CABIN

FRASER

BRITISH
WHITE PASS
DEAD HORSE COLUMBIA
GULCH ALASKA

GLACIER TUNNEL MT.

SKAGWAY
MILE 0

The Skagway dock in September, 1942—The docks were totally inadequate for the tons of materials that were flowing into the port from the south for shipment to Whitehorse via the railroad. USA

Troops boarding the train for Whitehorse—The passenger cars were left over from the days of the gold rush 42 years earlier. USA

Track of the White Pass and Yukon Railway, laid down Broadway Street in Skagway during the Gold Rush of 1898-1900, came to life again during World War II. AHL

Troops of Company B,
770th Railway Battalion
at Skagway, Alaska in
March, 1944.

DEDMAN'S PHOTO SHOP,
SKAGWAY, ALASKA

Summit of White
Pass, the bound-
ary between
Alaska and British
Columbia, 1944.
USA

Everybody had to help
dig the trains out in
winter. Rotary snow-
plows were effective
most of the time. USA

BRIDGES

One of the biggest problems the construction men encountered in building the Alaska Highway was bridging the many small streams and major rivers along the route. Over the entire stretch of highway 133 bridges and 8,000 culverts were built. Some of the streams could be crossed with small log structures but others were meandering glacier-fed rivers, hundreds of yards wide, that turned into raging torrents during spring breakup. Those rivers called for advanced bridge building techniques.

With the military necessity of opening the road as quickly as possible, temporary log or pontoon bridges were constructed over the smaller streams, and ferries were used on the larger rivers. The PRA personnel who followed to construct a more permanent road were to upgrade those bridges.

The Donjek River northwest of Kluane Lake was the most difficult of the rivers to cross. It is a wide, braided, glacial river that floods and produces major ice jams in the spring that play havoc with bridge abutments. The White River, 40 miles further up the road, is another raging, glacial river. Several successive log structures were stretched across the rivers but nothing was really satisfactory until permanent structures could be built.

The original Nisutlin Bay bridge at Teslin Lake was the longest trestle bridge constructed on the highway, stretching over 2,300 feet. The pilings for the foundations

Construction troops building one of the hundreds of bridges out of logs—Cross-cut saws were the power saws of the period. USA

were set on thin layers of sand in the river bottom, which was mostly solid ice.

The Peace River bridge at Taylor near Ft. St. John was the most difficult one to build. A ferry was used to carry the supplies across the river but it was inadequate for the quantity of material. A timber trestle bridge was built in October 1942, but the river destroyed it in November. A permanent steel bridge was started in December 1942 and completed in August 1943. It reached 2,130 feet in length. The river, however, was very treacherous in this area and it kept hammering at the piers until part of the bridge collapsed on Oct. 16, 1957. The government began to plan a new bridge at once and the present one was opened in January 1960.

After the Canadian Army assumed control of the highway in 1946, the first priorities were rebuilding some of the major bridges and replacing the hundreds of log culverts that had rotted through the years. The timber bridges over the large glacial rivers had to be replaced with the steel girder type, and today only one original bridge from the pioneer road remains, crossing Canyon Creek near Haines Junction.

The first bridge constructed across a stream was built with pontoons. The permanent log structure was constructed as soon as possible to facilitate two-way traffic and to have a strong structure to withstand the spring run-off. Pontoon bridges could be dismantled quickly and moved to another location. USA

Construction of the bridge across the White River. PABC

Primitive bridge construction. Notice the mosquito nets on some of the workers.
YA, HAYS COLLECTION

A completed log bridge over a stream. USA

Construction of the Peace River Bridge from the north
bank in April, 1943. The Peace is one of the great rivers
of northern Canada and fur trade traffic of the early
days moved on it. Millions of dollars in furs were
transported in giant canoes. The local ferry could not
handle the amount of supplies going up the road and a
suitable bridge had to be built. A timber trestle bridge
had been constructed across the river in October, 1942
but it did not withstand the raging river very long. NA

The Peace River Bridge near Ft. St. John, British Columbia—it was completed in August, 1943, 9 months after it
was started. It was the longest bridge on the highway at
2,130 feet and was built at a cost of four million dollars.
This was a major accomplishment for the continuous
use of the highway. This bridge met its end however on
Oct. 16, 1957, when the tremendous pressure of the
river forced the structure to collapse. The present
bridge was completed in January, 1960. PAA

Peace River Bridge, 1957. SPRHS

The Sikanni Chief Bridge at MP 159 is still standing but the highway has bypassed the old bridge. sc

The Sikanni Chief bridge—The first bridge was completely reconstructed in 1943. USA

Sikanni Chief Bridge, December, 1943. USA

Hundreds of bridges crossed the large rivers and small streams on the highway's 1,500 mile route. NA

Temporary bridges were built with the pioneer road construction. The PRA would come along later and build more permanent structures. GA and USA

A very primitive bridge across Canyon Creek. YA, KAMLOOPS MUSEUM COLLECTION

The only original bridge from 1942 still standing crosses
Canyon Creek at MP 996.3. SC

CAMP LIFE

*B*uilding a road in that remote part of the continent was very difficult for men and machines. The pressure to finish it as soon as possible did not leave much time for recreation or for admiring the scenery. It was a difficult situation for the thousands of men to be suddenly relocated to a hostile environment to fight the various problems of cold weather, inadequate living conditions, loneliness, insects, fatigue and dangerous construction methods. The black soldiers had an even more difficult time, as most of them were from the temperate climate of the lower 48 states and could not get used to the extreme sub-zero temperatures. Those men found recreation facilities even more scarce, but the troops did an admirable job while they were in the North Country.

Living conditions were particularly bad in the early period of construction. Men had to live in tents with inadequate heat in the winter and little insect protection in the summer. Supplying the food for such a large contingent of troops was a serious problem. As highway construction progressed, more suitable quarters were built and better food was obtained. In the winter, moose were abundant and provided a delightful alternative to the canned meat that was served.

Insects were a real problem in that area due to the large expanses of water used as breeding grounds. Head nets were very common—especially during the summer months, and many a worker was unable to work because of swelling from insect bites.

Cold weather was probably the hardest thing to become accustomed to. Most of the men had never experienced such extreme temperature ranges and in the worst of the cold it was very dangerous to work around the machines. Flesh could be frozen hard to metal, if touched, in a matter of seconds and ice water was always a hazard in building the bridges if one were to fall in.

In consideration of those adverse conditions, it is a tribute to the men that the highway was built in record time.

Home was where
one hung his hat.
SPRHS

Camp at Ft. St. John. GH

Worker's camp beside the Sikanni Chief Bridge, 1943. GA

Construction Camp at Watson Lake, Yukon Territory—the use of the portable, fast-erecting Quonset huts was widespread during the construction period. They were also warmer than the bell tents initially used. PABC

R.M. Smith construction camp at Dawson Creek, July, 1943. This was one of several Canadian contractors hired to work on the highway reconstruction. GA

Headquarters of the Public Roads Administration at Ft. St. John, 1943. GA

PRA living quarters at Ft. St. John. GA

Chow line for breakfast at a camp near Whitehorse in May, 1942. YA

Chow tables were built and then moved along with everything else each time a new campsite was established. The wide-brimmed campaign hats were used in the summer so mosquito nets could be draped over them to cover the head and shoulders. YA

Not only was the mosquito the scourge of the construction men, but the black fly, or as it was commonly called, "White Stockings" because of its white legs, also took its toll. The bites caused large swellings and much discomfort. NA

It was spring in the south but in the Yukon it was still winter on May 4, 1942 when three inches of snow fell on the tents of the 18th Engineers at Whitehorse. YA

Liard Hot Springs near MP 497 was a natural recreation spot just off the highway. It could warm up a person in a hurry even in the dead of winter. USA

Liard Hot Springs today has been developed and is maintained by the British Columbia government. USA

Camp set up near White River Junction, July, 1944. USA

Recreation facilities were limited by the remoteness and need for speed of construction. This is the 18th Engineers Regiment brass band giving a concert at the Silver City Camp on Kluane Lake on July 4, 1942. YA

Remains of Silver City, located on the south end of Kluane Lake, Yukon. It was founded in 1903 when gold was discovered on adjacent Silver Creek. For a time the town served as a stop on the Whitehorse and Kluane Road, which was incorporated into the Alaska Highway in 1942. During the building of the highway a construction camp was located here.
SC

TOWNS ALONG THE WAY

*T*he highway was built to connect Dawson Creek, British Columbia—the northern terminus of the Northern Alberta Railroad—with Fairbanks, Alaska, the largest city in interior Alaska. Between these two points (a distance of 1,550 miles) lay miles of seemingly endless forests, raging rivers, mountainous terrain and a few inhabited towns.

Before the war, Dawson Creek was a small town of approximately 600 people serving the rich farming area around it. It was named for Canadian geologist, George Dawson, who led a survey party through there in 1879. The railroad had been extended to that point in 1931. The town mushroomed to over three times its prewar size during the war years. A fire destroyed the center of town in February 1943.

Forty-seven miles north of Dawson Creek lies the town of Ft. St. John (MP 47, Km 75.6) originally established in 1806 on the banks of the Peace River as a trading post for the local Indians. The fur trade had been active in the area for many years. A Northwest Staging Route air base was established there in 1941 and the town began to grow.

Prince Rupert, British Columbia was an important port for the trans-shipment of supplies to Skagway. This is a view of the large U.S. Army camp on Acropolis Hill.

PHYLIS BOWMAN, PRINCE RUPERT, B.C.

The Canadian National Railroad extended to Prince Rupert on Canada's Pacific Coast.
PHYLIS BOWMAN, PRINCE RUPERT, B.C.

Three hundred miles northwest of Dawson Creek along a winter trail lies Ft. Nelson (MP 300, Km 482.7), an early fur trading post. Another Northwest Staging Route was built there and the town also began to grow.

The largest town along the highway route in Canada was Whitehorse (MP 919, Km 1,478.7), which had been spawned by the Klondike gold rush 45 years earlier. It was the northern terminus of the White Pass & Yukon Railway, which wound its way 110 miles north from Skagway, Alaska. It was also a supply point for the riverboats plying the Yukon River and the inland lakes of the Yukon. Whitehorse was a stop on the Northwest Staging Route which used the airport built there in 1929. The Northwest Service Command was established there in September 1942 to coordinate all supply, construction and defense operations of the United States Army in that part of Canada. The town also mushroomed in size during the war with the tons of materials pouring into the town and thousands of construction workers and soldiers stationed there.

There were several other towns and settlements along the route that were important. Watson Lake, Yukon Territory (MP 632, Km 1,016.9), was another Northwest Staging Route air base and a major center for highway construction. Lower Post, British Columbia (MP 620, Km 997.6), was an old Hudson's Bay Company trading post near the confluence of the Liard and Dease rivers, an early route for fur traders and prospectors.

Champagne, Yukon Territory (MP 974.7, Km 1,568.6), was another early trading post and Indian village established in 1902 on the famous Dalton Trail to the Klondike gold fields. Haines Junction, Yukon Territory (MP 1,016, Km 1,635.2), was established at the junction of the Haines Cutoff highway and the Alaska Highway. Silver City was an old ghost town on the south end of Kluane Lake in the Yukon. An old wagon road had been built from there to Whitehorse years earlier and the new highway followed part of it. Burwash Landing was established in 1904 on the north end of Kluane Lake as a trading post. Tok, Alaska (MP 1,314, Km 2,114.2), was established late in the 19th century and was the gateway to Alaska and Fairbanks. An important air base was established at Northway, Alaska early in the war. Delta Junction, Alaska (MP 1,422, Km 2,288), was established in 1918 as a construction camp on the Richardson Highway. Some consider that point the end of the Alaska Highway.

Fairbanks, in interior Alaska (MP 1,520, Km 2,445.7), was the final link in the highway and an important air base during the war. It was born of the gold rush in the early 1900s and established itself as the major city in interior Alaska. It was linked to the sea by the Alaska Railroad which stretched south to Anchorage. Its population swelled during the war with construction workers, soldiers and air force personnel who were stationed there to ready planes that were ferried up from the lower 48 states for shipment to Russia under the Lend Lease Act.

Tent town at Dawson Creek, early 1942. GA

The only liquor store in the Peace River country at Pounce Coupe, British Columbia a few miles east of Dawson Creek, 1942. GA

Dawson Creek, British Columbia in the 1940s—the town had a population of approximately 600 in 1942 and was the center of the great Peace River wheat country. By February, 1943 the town's population had mushroomed to over 1,600. In February, 1943 part of the center of town was destroyed by a dynamite explosion and fire. PAA

Supplies and equipment poured into Dawson Creek in early 1942 for the start of construction. SPRHS

Main Street of Dawson Creek, looking west. SPRHS

Main Street of Ft. St. John, August, 1942. Like other towns on the highway route and the Northwest Staging Route it was no longer an isolated village but an important site for the defense of Alaska and north-western Canada. GA

Aerial view of Ft. St. John, British Columbia—founded in 1806 as a trading post for the Sikanni Indians, it was a sleepy village until the Canadian government built an air base here in 1941, one of a string of bases from Edmonton to Fairbanks. The highway came through in 1942. NA

Headquarters camp at Ft. St. John, April, 1942. USA

Ft. Nelson, on the route of the new highway—The Hudson's Bay Company established a settlement here in 1800 on the banks of the Ft. Nelson River. A new town was constructed on the highway route. USA

View of Watson Lake just inside the Yukon border—One of the Northwest Staging Route's air bases was built there. The town became an important construction site along the highway. USA

The 18th Engineers Regimental Camp north of the Whitehorse airport in 1942—large tent cities were springing up along the highway route in the spring and summer of 1942 to house and feed the thousands of troops working on the road. Whitehorse was bursting at the seams with men and supplies in 1942. YA

Whitehorse, the head-
quarters for the Alaska
Highway, was one of the
main supply points and it
became a vast material
warehouse. From a prewar
population of 300, the town
expanded greatly during the
war years and was desig-
nated the permanent capitol
of the Yukon Territory in
1953. USA

Riverfront view of Whitehorse, 1944. USA

Aerial view of Whitehorse. YA, KAMLOOPS MUSEUM COLLECTION

Main Street in Whitehorse in the 1940s—Many things have changed in the past four decades. USA

The liquor store in Whitehorse must have been the most popular place in town for the soldiers and civilian construction workers on their few days off. YA

Burwash Landing on Kluane Lake in years past had been a base for hunting parties going into the Kluane area of the Yukon. It was a base for soldiers of the United States Army Corps of Engineers during the highway construction. NA

Fairbanks, Alaska in December, 1943 at the northern terminus of the highway—Fairbanks was an old gold mining town from the early 1900s and during the war became very important in the defense of Alaska. USA

Carcross, Yukon on Lake Bennett was an important stop on the White Pass and Yukon for both highway construction and the CANOL pipeline project. The Caribou Hotel in the background is still standing. YA, FINNIE COLLECTION

Wartime scenes of Broadway Avenue in Skagway, Alaska, an important shipping port for the highway and CANOL project. YA, FINNIE COLLECTION

RECONSTRUCTION

*T*he pioneer road had been punched through the wilderness in record time. But in early 1943 the PRA had the job of upgrading the road to a year around passable condition with widths of 26 to 32 feet. Grades had to be reduced and straightened, new roadbeds had to be built across the many swampy sections and permanent bridges had to be built. That was no easy task and the same problems that faced the builders of the pioneer road also faced the PRA men.

As the original construction regiments were pulled off the project in early to mid 1943, private contractors were hired by the PRA to do the reconstruction. Although the PRA had been on the job since its inception, more than 16,000 civilian construction workers employed by American and Canadian companies were now on the job. PRA offices were set up in Ft. St. John and Whitehorse to direct the construction, with other small offices scattered along the route.

Five major contractors were hired to oversee the construction. Each in turn subcontracted with individual companies for certain parts of the job. In addition, highly technical contractors were hired for the large bridge projects. No one had any idea how long it was to take to bring the road up to a standard for safe travel due to the many variables of weather and supply problems.

More than 70 companies were involved in the reconstruction project. But by October 1943, with the military situation improving in the Pacific area and the highway upgraded as an all-weather road, the government ordered the project completed. Thousands of men and tons of material and machines started to move to the "outside." The army then took over and did what maintenance it could to keep the road open.

They left the legacy of an overland route to Alaska and northern Canada that has vastly changed the country.

The total cost of the road was over $138 million and required the placement of 133 bridges and 8,000 culverts.

LEONARD VANDENBERG,
KALAMAZOO, MICHIGAN

Utah Construction Company equipment improved the grade and alignment of the pioneer road by Goose Bay, Kluane Lake. The bulldozer in the foreground is keeping the road open to traffic. The other equipment is making a cut directly across the road just ahead of the bulldozer in the foreground; at the same time the equipment is using the material to build a fill in the clearing over the culvert to the right, August, 1943. NA

One bulldozer pulling out another stuck at Slana, Alaska in July, 1943. USA

A command car stuck in the mud near the White River in May, 1943. NA

Even the base camp at Dawson Creek was susceptible to the ever present scourge of mud. GA

Aerial view showing reconstruction of the original pioneer road in September, 1943—a multitude of tracks have been made by trucks and equipment attempting to fight their way through this swampy section. The original road cannot be isolated in the confusion of trails. NA

The highway snakes its way through the Rancheria Valley in the Yukon. The road bisects some of the most beautiful and rugged terrain in North America. In parts it curved a great deal due to the many swampy areas that had to be avoided. The first road was strictly a pioneer road. It was left to the follow-up crews to straighten that one out and improve on it. PABC

Icing a corduroy section of road near Swift River, February, 1943. When the water froze it would provide a smooth surface over the rough logs. YA, FINNIE COLLECTION

PRA equipment frozen in a bar of the Donjek River in February, 1942. NA

The ever-present mud was a constant problem along much of the highway. SPRHS

Equipment boneyard near Teslin, Yukon, February, 1943.
YA, FINNIE COLLECTION

A long truck convoy along one of the dry sections of the road.
SPRHS

The reconstruction of the army's pioneer road was completed at this spot on Oct. 13, 1943 by the Utah Construction Company, a private contractor working for the PRA. NA

Canadian civilian construction workers of the Department of Mines and Resources between Ft. St. John and Ft. Nelson. GA

Trucks carrying dynamite caps, Dawson Creek area, July, 1943. GA

All traffic on the highway had to be authorized by the army for security and safety reasons. This was the check-in station at Dawson Creek, British Columbia at the start of the highway. NA

V-E Day celebration on a baseball field in Whitehorse in 1945—The highway had served well in the defense of Alaska and Canada. USA

Not only did the highway open up the North Country for motorized traffic but it afforded the native people easier access to the outside world. NA

HAINES CUTOFF ROAD

*T*he Haines Cutoff road was authorized by the United States Army in November 1942 as the Alaska Pioneer Road was being finished. The cutoff was to be built to link the port of Haines, Alaska with the Alaska Highway, a distance of 160 miles. It was also built to provide an alternate route to the highway in case the White Pass and Yukon Railway was blocked, to provide another port for the shipment of supplies to the highway, and to provide a possible mass evacuation route from Alaska in case that became necessary.

The road took almost one year to build—from January to December 1943—at a cost of over $13 million. The road traverses the rugged country on the east side of the St. Elias Range through parts of Alaska, British Columbia and the Yukon Territory.

Some of the same construction difficulties encountered on the Alaska Highway were also met on the Cutoff road, but much had been learned on the original pioneer road. Camps were built along the route for the construction workers. Major camps were at 103 mile and at Dezadeash Lake.

In the winter of 1944, the United States Army discontinued the winter maintenance of the road, and the Canadian portion was returned to the Canadian Army after the end of the war.

Bus service was instituted along the highway by the Northwest Service Command to carry passengers between Dawson Creek and Whitehorse. SPRHS

POST CONSTRUCTION

*B*y 1943 the threat of a Japanese invasion had waned due to reversals on all war fronts in the Pacific. The need for the highway was not as critical as during the early days of 1942. The United States Army was responsible for maintenance of the road but by 1944, the work force was reduced to between 300 and 500 men (all Canadian civilians). The idea of building an all-weather highway with high standards was abandoned for the time being and only essential relocation work was authorized, with all work by the PRA to be phased out by the end of October 1943.

The problems encountered by the initial construction crews were inherited by the civilian workers, especially the icing conditions and washouts. Bridges were a continual problem, dozens were washed out in 1943 and 1944. It was a constant battle to keep the highway open with the adverse weather conditions, limited funding and manpower.

Six months after the war was over the Americans were to turn the highway over to Canadian authorities. In April 1946, the Royal Canadian Army officially took over operation and maintenance of the road. There was little usable construction equipment left, and only a small work force to oversee the 1,200 miles of road in Canada. There was an immediate need to upgrade the road and bridges, as there was pressure to open the road to civilian use.

Civilian traffic was restricted in 1946 and 1947. The road was opened for a time in 1948, but had to close because of the high number of car breakdowns. By 1949 the highway was opened on a full-time basis with tourist facilities being expanded every year thereafter. April 1, 1964 saw the highway's military administration come to an end and the Department of Public Works took over the Canadian portion of the road. The Alaska portion was maintained by the Alaska Road Commission.

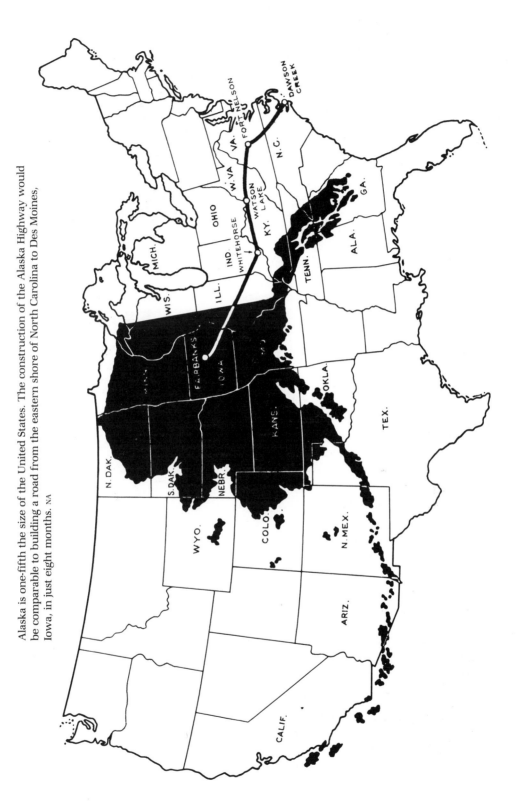

Alaska is one-fifth the size of the United States. The construction of the Alaska Highway would be comparable to building a road from the eastern shore of North Carolina to Des Moines, Iowa, in just eight months. NA

WATSON LAKE SIGNPOSTS
by Carl Lindley, Danville, Illinois

*O*n the west end of the Watson Lake, Yukon townsite is a forest of signposts from just about every corner of the globe. The story of its beginning goes back to 1943 during the construction days of the Alaska Highway. It is told here by Carl Lindley of Danville, Illinois, who was a soldier with Company D, 341st Engineers, who were working on the highway:

"I had received an injury near the border of British Columbia and Yukon, north of Lower Post. My foot was mashed while building a loading platform to fill dump trucks. I was taken to the Company aid station at nearby Watson Lake where I spent three weeks convalescing. Unable to do much work the C.O. asked me if I could repair and repaint the sign that was partially destroyed by bulldozers. From the nature of the sign, I was encouraged to add my own version and added a sign to Danville, Illinois my hometown."

From this one sign of a homesick GI's hometown, the sign forest has expanded to over 6,000 stretched along the Alaska Highway in front of the Yukon Government's new Alaska Highway Interpretive Center. It is one of the best known attractions along the 1,500 mile highway from Dawson Creek, British Columbia to Fairbanks, Alaska.

SIGN FOREST—FIRST SIGN

ALASKA HIGHWAY WATSON LAKE

AT 635 MILE MARKER

NEW YORK 3600 mi

CHICAGO 2700

EDMONTON 1215 ml

LOWER POST 15½ mls

WATSON LAKE 8 miles

LIARD RIVER 8 miles

WHITEHORSE 322

TESLIN 172 miles

TOKYO 4000 air miles

FIRST SIGN   © 1978 CARL LINDLEY

Carl Lindley at Upper Liard River.

GOVERNMENT OF THE YUKON

Monument to 1st Lt. R.R. Small, Co F 18th Engineer Regiment who died in the line of duty on August 9, 1942. sc

The Alaska Highway Interpretive Center at Watson Lake, Yukon, operated by the Yukon Government. sc

GERTRUDE

ED KERRY AND "GERTRUDE", HIS 1938 INTERNATIONAL
TD 35 TRACTOR, CAME TO THE YUKON AS A TEAM
IN THE 1940'S DURING THE BUILDING OF THE ALASKA
HIGHWAY. GERTRUDE'S ACCOMPLISHMENTS SPANNED 40
YEARS, AND INCLUDE CONSTRUCTION OF AIRSTRIPS, CITY
STREETS IN WHITEHORSE, PORTIONS OF THE ALASKA
HIGHWAY, AND CONSTRUCTION SITES ALL OVER THE YUKON.
"GERTIE" WAS DONATED TO THE YUKON GOVERNMENT BY
THE KERRY FAMILY IN MEMORY OF ED KERRY, A LOYAL
AND TRUE YUKONER.

Some of the
original road can
still be found but
most has been
obliterated by new
construction
through the years.
SC

Concrete pad of a
building built in
1943 at the Big
Creek Camp-
ground near Wat-
son Lake. SC

Mile '0' at Dawson Creek, British Columbia. sc

The end of the highway at Delta Junction, Alaska. From here the highway connected with the existing Richardson Highway to Fairbanks. sc

Members of the 340th Engineers. PHOTOS FROM DOROTHY JONES, FOREST GROVE, OREGON

"Home Sweet Home," spring 1942.

Members of Co D 341st Engineers.

Cutting timbers for a bridge, Upper
Liard River.

ABOUT THE AUTHOR

Stan Cohen is a native of West Virginia and a graduate geologist from West Virginia University. After spending years as a consulting geologist, owner of a ski business and director of a historical park, he established Pictorial Histories Publishing Company in 1976. He has written 35 books and published over 75. Cohen has made 17 trips over the Alaska Highway in the past 25 years pursuing his interest in the highway's history. Cohen lives in Missoula, Montana, with his wife, Anne, and son, Andy.

Alaska/Canada books by Stan Cohen:

The Streets Were Paved with Gold—A Pictorial History of the Klondike Gold Rush, 1896-99.

The Forgotten War—A Pictorial History of World War II in Alaska and Northwestern Canada.

The Forgotten War—A Pictorial History of World War II in Alaska and Northwestern Canada, Volume II.

Rails Across the Tundra—A Pictorial History of the Alaska Railroad.

Gold Rush Gateway—Skagway and Dyea, Alaska.

Yukon River Steamboats—A Pictorial History.

The Great Alaska Pipeline.

Flying Beats Work—The Story of Reeve Aleutian Airways

White Pass and Yukon Route—A Pictorial History

Queen City of the North—Dawson City, Yukon

Alaska books from Pictorial Histories:

Alaska Wilderness Rails, by Ken Brovald

Top Cover for America, by John Cloe

The Opening of Alaska, by Brig. Gen. Billy Mitchell

Journey to the Koyukuk—The Photos of J.N. Wyman.

Write for complete descriptions and catalog.

The Trail of '42 video available.
60 minutes of historical and contemporary footage.
$29.95 US, $34.95 CDN, plus $1.50 postage.

PICTORIAL HISTORIES PUBLISHING COMPANY
713 South Third Street West, Missoula, Montana 59801
Phone: (406) 549-8488